THE BEATITUDES

LARGE PRINT EDITION

ROBERT HOWIE FISHER

ALICIA EDITIONS

CONTENTS

PREFACE

In "The Beatitudes," we are privileged to present a profound and inspiring work by Robert Howie Fisher. As a publisher committed to disseminating meaningful and transformative literature, we believe that this book will undoubtedly leave a lasting impact on its readers.

The Beatitudes, spoken by Jesus Christ during the Sermon on the Mount, have transcended time and cultural barriers, resonating with seekers of truth across generations. Fisher's eloquent exploration of these eight blessings opens a gateway to a deeper understanding of their timeless relevance in today's complex world.

Robert Howie Fisher, a prominent figure in the 19th century Scottish religious landscape, was born in 1861. From an early age, he displayed a deep curiosity about religious matters and embarked on a lifelong journey of exploring the sacred scriptures and Christian teachings. Fisher's thirst for knowledge led him to pursue theological studies, and he soon became recognized as a gifted preacher and spiritual writer.

Through meticulous research and thoughtful analysis, Fisher unveils the profound layers of wisdom contained within each Beatitude. From the call to embrace humility and meekness to the invitation to seek righteousness and make peace, the book invites readers on a soul-stirring journey of self-discovery and spiritual growth.

Fisher's unique blend of scholarly insight and heartfelt reflection brings a refreshing perspective to these ancient teachings. His approach goes beyond mere academic analysis, providing practical applications that empower readers to embody the Beatitudes in their daily lives.

We commend Fisher for his dedication to presenting the Beatitudes in a way that is accessible to both clergy and laity alike. As we navigate the complexities of modern existence, the wisdom found within this book serves as a guiding light for individuals seeking purpose, authenticity, and a deeper connection with their faith.

This volume is a testament to the power of spiritual exploration and the significance of the Beatitudes in nurturing the human soul. As a publisher, we are honored to play a role in sharing this timeless message with a global audience, inviting readers to embrace the transformative potential of the Beatitudes in their personal and communal lives.

We express our gratitude to our readers for their continuous support in our mission to offer literature that enriches lives and inspires positive change.

May this book, "The Beatitudes," be a source of inspiration and illumination for all who embark on its pages. May it lead readers towards a more profound understanding of their own spirituality and encourage them to live out the blessings proclaimed by Christ in their daily endeavors.

Alicia EDITIONS

CHAPTER I
THE POOR IN SPIRIT

"Blessed are the poor in spirit: for theirs is the kingdom of heaven."

— ST. MATT. V. 3.

When St. Luke recorded the Beatitudes he rendered this saying, "Blessed be ye poor" — poor without qualification — "for yours is the kingdom of God." The critics have discussed which was the original form of the Beatitude, most of them inclining to the shorter and simpler form.

But is there, indeed, any reason why Jesus should not have expressed the thought in both ways? If critics would only keep near to the experience of life they would be saved from many difficulties. Every preacher and teacher is for ever repeating and reiterating favourite thoughts, modifying them in expression as occasion requires, believing that such repetition is the only way to permanent impression. At one time, and to a wider audience than the disciples (as St. Luke suggests), our Lord may have said, "Blessed be ye poor" — poor in purse and possession. And the multitude who heard — remember that the great majority of mankind are poor — would not misunderstand His message. They would recognise the universal note in it — its large democratic reference. As a poor man spoke to poor men, they would see that their lot was not without its alleviations.

It was not the first time that a prophet of Israel had given a warning against the risks of riches — the danger of self-complacency and arrogance and materialism, the danger of supposing that because out of a superfluity it is easy to do kind and good things, therefore one is a kind and good man. Nor was it the first time that a prophet of Israel had declared that the grace of God, and all the things which matter most for life, cannot be bought for money, and are independent of outward conditions. "The poor have the gospel preached to them," was as much the burden of Isaiah as of our Lord.

One need not doubt, therefore, that at some time — or it may be often — Jesus spoke to the masses of men and said, without any qualification or more inward meaning, "Blessed be ye poor."

Yet He gave to the disciples — He left for us — a

message far more profound than that. Jesus would have been the last to limit spiritual graces to any outward lot. All beggars are not like Lazarus. A poor man may be as grasping and avaricious and material as any millionaire. Moreover, there was in the history of His people the record of men of wealth — men like Abraham and Job, who were reverenced by their race as men of God. In His own teaching our Lord dwelt much on the right stewardship of property; and He offered the noblest reward that service ever gained to the man who had wisely turned his five talents into ten. He, who knew human nature through and through, understood well how a certain measure of comfort saves from many of the grosser temptations of life, and how wealth increases the chances of usefulness which are open to a generous and unselfish man. Most of us can only follow one profession — we are doctors, or lawyers, or teachers, or so forth. But a rich man can follow many professions. His money can endow research, can found hospitals, can multiply libraries, museums, galleries of art. Vicariously, by his wealth, he can be the general benefactor of mankind. It is obvious to any one who knows the teaching of Christ that He recognised this, and would have been ill-content had His blessing been withheld from the philanthropist of the warm heart and liberal hand.

It is probable, therefore, that the Beatitude as St. Matthew has recorded it — whether or not it be the first form or the form most commonly used — is the profoundest expression of the mind of Christ. It alone is wholly true to His method of inwardness; it alone makes plain that it is not a man's possessions or his poverty that matters, it is the man himself. "Blessed are the poor in spirit" — whether they are poor in pocket or not.

When we read the Beatitude in this form we see within its folds two most characteristic teachings of our Lord.

I. The first is the worth of mere manhood and womanhood. Whether men and women be rich or poor, high or low, learned or ignorant, they yet are men and women: and their wisdom is to reverence their nature as a thing apart from all adventitious considerations. If he learn this lesson aright, the wealthiest man may be "poor in spirit."

It is evident from this that the grace of the Beatitude is as far remote as can be from what is called "poor-spiritedness" — from the frame of the mean and timid, or from defective spirituality. Only a man accomplished in the life of the soul is able to see himself apart from his surroundings and to face the naked reality of things. It was one of the great charms of the Stoic temper — it was the Stoic's contribution to the philosophy of life — that an emperor like Marcus Aurelius and a slave like Epictetus were alike able to see past the accidents of life to the essential worth of the human soul. What Jesus meant by being "poor in spirit," was just this Stoic discernment of the big and meaningful beside those outward possessions which loom so large in the eyes of many who have not learned the proportion of things.

A great Christian divine, Jeremy Taylor, set forth the same lesson when he wrote: "I have fallen into the hands of thieves: what then? They have left me the sun and the moon, fire and water, a loving wife, and many friends to pity me, and some to relieve me, and I can still discourse. And, unless I list, they have not taken away my merry countenance and my cheerful spirit and a good conscience."

The patriarch Job, long before either the Stoic or the Christian teacher, had spoken the language of the poor in spirit in words more memorable than any when he said, "The Lord gave, and the Lord hath taken away: blessed be the name of the Lord."

It is impossible not to admire those who can sit so lightly to outward conditions, and who can be themselves alike in sunshine and in shower. Yet the question arises: Are we to agree with those who maintain that such an attitude is impossible for ourselves, and the grace of the Beatitude is so unworldly that it is for ever beyond our reach?

Such "poverty of spirit" is not so uncommon an accomplishment as such sceptics would suppose. Every one remembers how Dr. Johnson went to see the famous actor David Garrick in his rooms, and as he looked on Garrick's surroundings of luxury and beauty and artistic value, he said, "Ah, Davie, Davie, these are the things which make death terrible." But though a casual spectator of such an attractive environment might without foolishness utter such a sentiment, one wonders how far it entered at all into the facts of the case, and whether a man like Garrick was less able and willing to see the naked truths of the world than if his abode had been amid objects less congenial to his artistic nature.

It is likely to be true that a man will learn to be "poor in spirit" most readily just when he is least occupied with external considerations; and that is when his surroundings jar the least upon his sensibilities. Here is for ever the justification of fine art.

For the same reason one has little belief in the crusade of those daring spirits who advocate what they call the "simple life." Grant all the elements of force in their plea, there remains the insuperable objection that their attitude is a pose, an affectation, an aping of self-sacrifice. What they attain of outward conformity to the simple life, they lose in real simplicity of spirit. The inwardness of the Beatitude is at enmity with every artificial counterfeit.

Yet in all classes of the community there are multitudes who attain to its spirit — multitudes who are not troubling much about what they have or can gain, who are more interested in the friendships and affections with which they are surrounded, the books they read, the causes in which they are absorbed, their political party, their Church — external things, no doubt, yet not incompatible with "poverty of spirit," not leading to self-assertion or arrogance, not thought of as personal possessions, but as the innocent preoccupation of unworldly souls.

So far from the first Beatitude enshrining an unattainable grace, the genuine humility of it is the normal frame of mind, at least of the majority of thinking men and women. Most people know that they came naked into this world, and are near an inevitable hour when they will go naked out of it

II. It is when we turn to a second and more religious meaning of the Beatitude that one is less certain of its common attainment. Not only do the "poor in spirit" know that the things which are seen and temporal are the accidents and not the essentials of life; they know also that, because they are poor, they need to depend on God. To be humble and to feel one's helplessness is one thing; to look above for help is another. The Stoic did not learn that second lesson; and in the presence of proofs of our weakness in the universe more appalling than any Stoic ever realised, there are thousands of our fellow-countrymen who will not learn it.

> "Nothing in my hand I bring.
> Simply to Thy Cross I cling;
> Naked, come to Thee for
> dress;
> Helpless, look to Thee for
> grace."

That is the complete utterance of him who is "poor in spirit." At the Holy Communion he says, "We are not worthy so much as to gather the crumbs that fall from Thy Table." His very attitude at prayer asserts his dependence. When he offers alms he says, with King David, "All things come of Thee, and of thine own we give Thee." When he goes forth to Christian service he knows how true were the words of His Master, "Without me ye can do nothing." Truth, holiness, happiness — for all he depends on Another. He is a little child in the great Father's house, and knows that for the provision of body and mind and spirit he looks to the Father's bounty.

That is a difficult grace to learn. But until we have learned to be dependent on God, as well as independent of the world, we have not earned the whole blessing upon the "poor in spirit."

III. A third reflection remains. It is that here we have the best light on our Lord's use of rewards and punishments. "Blessed are the poor in spirit: for theirs is the kingdom of heaven."

There is no use in denying that many moralists and religious thinkers have been distressed by the feet that the New Testament seems so full of the idea of gain. Do this, and you will be amply paid for it. Deny yourself that, and a rich compensation will anon await you. The Evangelical preachers of another day — not so far remote from ours — were most forcible when they expounded such a theme, and made heaven or hell the alluring or deterrent incentives to conduct. They were not without their appeal to the very words of Jesus — to such blessings as those of the first Beatitude, and to such promises as were made to the Twelve Disciples, that if they forsook houses and lands for Christ's sake, manifold more of outward blessings would be theirs even in this world, and an eternal guerdon of glory would crown their heads beyond.

The modern mind has turned from such an estimate of virtue as conduct calculated by consequence, and sees the only worth of virtue in its being sought for itself alone. A writer like the late Sir John Seeley made out that the disciples of our Lord, if they believed His promises, were really making an astute bargain for themselves, and the veneration which the Church has paid them would on such a basis be little enough deserved.

But surely in these very Beatitudes is the key to all our Saviour's use of rewards and punishments. At times our Lord spoke of material things. In a world of imagery He had to speak in images. The streets of gold and the many mansions of the Father's house seemed a wonderful reward to a poor man with his one-roomed house. Yet all the time Christ's mind was dominated with other and spiritual things, and every symbol must be read in the light of the Sermon on the Mount, with its promises for the spirit alone. Applause, indeed, is the due of virtue; reward is its proper flower and crown. "Blessed are the poor in spirit: for theirs is the kingdom of heaven." But the only reward worth thinking of is the joy of going on. Even now the "poor in spirit" enter the atmosphere of the eternal, and some breath of their immortal destiny fans their brow. They know even now that they are not mocked; that their aspirations are not in vain; that they are not seeking an illusion which will vanish as one has seen the mirage of the desert vanish as experience brought a nearer view. Theirs is, and because it *is, will be* the Kingdom of Heaven. Fancy telling a scientific man that his reward will be some money, some tide, some popularity. The reward he seeks is to learn more of nature, to seek more firmly the control of her agencies, to wrest something more of her secret out of the dark. Fancy telling a good man that his reward will be to sit on a gold throne, and to play a harp for all eternity. The reward he seeks is to know himself better — to see faculties he has hardly as yet realised develop and gain co-ordination and elasticity and power; it is to see a usefulness which he had dreamed of, but which narrow limits of opportunity had restricted, become great and beneficent on an ampler field in a serener air; it is to find a fellowship open and generous, and ever widening and deepening with the holy, wise, and good, who are the true congeners of his soul. Such a reward — not selfish or sordid or unworthy of the loftiest of our race — Jesus has promised to His people. "Blessed are the poor in spirit: for theirs is the kingdom of heaven."

CHAPTER 2
THE MOURNERS

"Blessed are they that mourn: for they shall be comforted."

—ST. MATT. V. 4

An eminent teacher has said: "It will ever be a question whether men abuse more their sorrows or their joys; but no earnest soul can doubt which of these abuses is the more fatal. To sin in the one case is to yield to a temptation: to sin in the other is to resist a divine grace. Sorrow is God's last message to man. It is God speaking in emphasis. He who abuses it shows that he can shut his ears when God speaks loudest." There are few people who can read such words without some measure of self-reproach. A man who has gone through great trouble said to the present writer that "he knew that he was a better man before it. It had done him no good." If we are entirely honest with ourselves we shall probably all admit that we have lost much through our sorrows — lost a certain buoyancy and elasticity of life which will not come back again, and an interest in the world and in our kind which was one of our happiest possessions.

If indeed our sorrow has been that which St Paul described as the "sorrow of the world," it has injured us still more deeply. If we have met it heartlessly, trying only to divert our minds from it by amusement or self-indulgence or the quips of a cynical humour, then it has only hardened and soured our nature. That sorrow of the world worketh death.

But even at the best, even when it was godly sorrow, many will admit that it has chilled them. So far from the conventional phrases about "refiner's fire" being completely true, the furnace of affliction has not left our nature pure gold. If some dross has gone, some cinders and some smoke of the fire are clinging to us.

There is no matter in which absolute truthfulness, both with ourselves and towards those whom we would fain help in their time of trouble, is more necessary than in the matter of consolation, and especially in the use of the comforts of religion. A false note jars and hurts like a blow. Therefore, even when we hear our Lord say, "Blessed are they that mourn: for they shall be comforted," we remember that He did not say that such comfort makes up for everything, and that there is no blessing also for the unharassed life. Blessed are they who know the joy of the Lord.

This needs to be said by way of caution. Every one cannot reflect on a past sorrow as Cardinal Newman did —

> "I would not miss one sigh or
>   tear,
>   Heart-pang or throbbing
>   brow;
> Sweet was the agony severe,
>   And sweet its memory
>   now."

Yet that would be a strange soul who could not understand the Lord's Beatitude on mourning, and who met it with no acquiescence and belief. However little satisfied we are with the gait in which we passed through the Dark Valley, at least we have brought three things out of it

I. The first is a kindlier view of our fellows. One uses homely words, and says, "I never knew people were so good before." That is about comparative strangers. Then there were the hearts nearer our own, about whom we felt that they were really suffering with us in our trouble, giving virtue out of themselves that somehow they might relieve and strengthen us. Thus even in our bitterest hours we felt that the cords of love were being more tightly drawn.

> "Mortal, if thou art beloved,
> Life's offences are removed.
> All the fateful things that
>   checked thee,
> Hearten, hallow, and protect
>   thee.
> What is sorrow? Comfort's
>   prime;
> Love's choice Indian Summer
>   time.
> Sickness! thou wilt pray it
>   worse,
> For so blessed kindly nurse.
> And for Death! when thou art
>   dying,
> 'Twill be Love beside thee
>   lying."

There can be no doubt at all that it is in the Dark Valley of mourning, and not on the happy plains of life, that the best sides of human nature are revealed, and we learn also to believe in that Divine Love which came to its climax of tenderness on a Cross. Therefore, "Blessed are they that mourn."

II. A second gain that comes from sorrow is an added sense of the seriousness of life. We may not think ourselves better men or women after it, but certainly we are more thoughtful. Sorrow may not do everything; but it sobers the judgment, and makes us see ourselves and the world with clearer eyes. These were true words which George Eliot wrote of one of her characters: "Adam Bede had not outlived his sorrow — had not felt it slip from him as a temporary burden, and leave him the same man again. Do any of us? God forbid. It would be a poor result of all our anguish and our wrestling if we won nothing but our old selves at the end of it, if we could return to the same blind loves, the same self-confident blame, the same light thoughts of human suffering, the same frivolous gossip over blighted human lives, the same feeble sense of the unknown towards which we have sent forth irrepressible cries in our loneliness." Some such blessing of seriousness must ever be brought by mourning. A common word we use has a wonderful suggestion of this in it. We talk of a "heavy sorrow" — never of a heavy joy. Joy is light and bubbles up. But sorrow sounds the deeps. It takes a man to the bed - rock of experience. Because it is always good to be in contact with real-ity, there is a blessedness in mourning which hardly comes in happier days.

Think, for example, how it makes a man know the worth of his religion — sometimes with ap-palling distress when he discovers that familiar and accepted phrases have no potency to cheer; and sometimes with a sweet wonder that he had never understood before the graciousness of the promises of God. If, while the sun shone, the profoundest things of life had thus been unseen and unrealised, like the stars at noonday, was it not a blessing when, with the thick darkness, "Hesperus and the host of heaven came, and lo, creation widened to our view"?

III. Those who search their own experience for the meaning of sorrow will not deny a third blessing which it brings. It gives a chance of making something great of life. Most people, with moderate abilities and a restricted career, go through the world with few impulses to spiritual development. Their life is dull, not because it is empty, but because the incidents which people it are so little varied from each other. Few occasions call for the self-denials and heroisms which give their colour to character and fix the levels on which life is to be led. A great sorrow is such an occasion — perhaps the most stimulating which men and women know. Every latent resource is summoned to effectiveness, and commonplace people discover that the inspiration which makes shipwreck or war or pestilence call out the noblest that is in humanity is bearing its romance even to them.

If we could always live at the levels which we gain at such hours of grief, how much larger would be our minds, how much more generous our hopes and aims! A husband and a father said beside the dead body of his child, "We must try to have a more religious home after this." One realised that sorrow was (awaking in the man aspirations and affinities ' which might — if the glory did not fade — make him enter upon fields of spiritual experience hitherto untravelled, and embrace for his own a life of piety and benevolence which would be the manifest confirmation of the Beatitude, "Blessed are they that mourn."

Thus in the revelation which our trouble makes of human brotherliness, in the deepened gravity of thought which it induces, and in its summons to heroism and godliness, the compensations of sorrow may be found, and mourning may truly be called blessed.

But surely the very fact that consolation is promised, and the mourners pronounced blessed because they shall be comforted, is in itself a proof that mourning is not the normal nor the highest condition of the soul. Even now, in this world of pain, surcease of sorrow is promised to all those who love the Lord. "Come unto Me all ye that labour and are heavy laden, and I will give you rest." "My peace I give unto you." "Enter ye into the joy of your Lord." And, in the world to come, it is the promise of the Blessed Home that there "God shall wipe away all tears from their eyes, and there shall be no more death, neither sorrow, nor crying, neither shall there be any more pain; for the former things have passed away."

In presence of such invitations and promises — in the light of our knowledge of human character — it is necessary to attempt some reconciliation of the blessing upon the mourners with the description of the highest and the lasting life as a life of joy. Such a reconciliation is found in the career of our Lord Jesus Christ Bishop Gore has finely said: "The character which we find described in the Beatitudes is beyond all question nothing else than our Lord's own character put into words... It is a description set side by side with an example." Now, our Lord is called the "Man of Sorrows," and we know how truly the world's sorrow broke His heart Yet He was also a man of joy. The complete fulfilment of duty brought Him delight, the peace of domestic affection charmed Him: He found amid the hills and by the sea "the joy of elevated thoughts." Which title, the man of sorrows, or the man of joy, bears the truest revelation of His nature? Are not both titles in themselves inadequate to represent a complete ideal? And is not the full truth about Him this — that He knew well that

> "Not enjoyment and not
> sorrow
> Is our destined end and way."

As a man upon a journey, He smiled gladly when the sun shone; and He strode on unmurmuringly when the rain fell: but He was not out to enjoy the weather; He was on an errand; and whatever were the conditions He met, He was master of Himself and of them — not "the man of

Pleasure," not "the man of Pain": but "the man of Power."

Such a detachment is the secret of a final victory, both over sorrow and over happiness, and of the Beatitude both upon the mourners and upon those who rejoice. Tolstoi has put it well: "A man who lives a Christian life does not ascribe any great meaning to his joys, but looks on them as accidental phenomena which meet him in the path of life. And he does not look upon his sufferings as something that ought not to be. He looks on them as indispensable phenomena of life, like friction at work." If that be true — and the final pattern of human character be neither crowned with flowers nor draped in black, but a large humane spirit which finds itself at home in every vicissitude — like a good ship making her way homeward-bound through all seas — we need not linger exclusively and overmuch on the Beatitude upon the mourners, as if they alone were blessed. Our wisdom is to extract the lesson from every event and see the Providence of all the discipline of our lives. Though a man should study at a university many years and gain many and high degrees, he would not have found a fuller philosophy of life than that which St. Paul had discovered for himself while he tried to follow his Master: "I have learned, in whatsoever state I am, therewith to be content. I know both how to be abased and I know how to abound. Everywhere and in all things I am instructed both to be full and to be hungry, both to abound and to suffer need. I can do all things through Christ which strengtheneth me." That is indeed the true wisdom of a full-orbed life. All else is one-sided.

Once when the celebrated French preacher Massillon was preaching before Louis xiv. he addressed the King directly, as was the unseemly custom of the time, and said, "If the world addressed your majesty from this place, the world would not say, 'Blessed are they that mourn,' but blessed is the prince who has never fought but to conquer, who has filled the universe with his name, who through the whole course of a long and flourishing reign enjoys in splendour all that men admire — extent of conquest, the esteem of enemies, the love of his people, the wisdom of his laws. But, sire, the language of the Gospel is not the language of the world." Yet if the world had been speaking the truth and not gross flattery in such an address, the world would have been nearer than the preacher to the large sane wisdom of St. Paul and of his Lord, who saw the experiences of life in their due place, in their right proportion, and could find a wholesome happiness in the hour of triumph as well as in the hour of defeat. There is no deprecation of the blessedness of fine achievement in the assurance that failure also, rightly encountered, will yield its blessedness; "Blessed are they that mourn, for they shall be comforted."

CHAPTER 3
THE MEEK

"Blessed are the meek: for they shall inherit the earth."

— ST. MATT. V. 5.

No virtue is more easily counterfeited than meekness. But most assuredly the blessing which belongs to the real virtue is not promised to the counterfeit.

I. Men may be meek for gain. A prudent regard for self-interest will check the expression of their own opinion and repress the outburst of their temper. And they will be meek because they must. It would not pay a shopman, harassed as he often is by unreasonable customers, to betray his annoyance or his amusement. So must a subordinate often accept without a murmur the petty irritation of his superior, finding relief for his feelings, perhaps, in passing on the unpleasantness to some one who in turn is subordinate to him. People have often to learn the truth of that saying of Queen Elizabeth to one of her courtiers who had been goaded into an ill-tempered retort. "Ah, Sir Philip," "anger often makes men witty; but it always keeps them poor." The meekness of manner which is trained by such self-interest is a poor enough imitation of the Christian grace which our Master declared to be blessed.

II. But it is better than another counterfeit which passes for meekness — the placidity of temper whose mother is disdain. There are some composed, unruffled natures whose only motive for self-restraint is that they do not think it worth while to show any feeling. A genuine contempt for the judgment of their neighbours is the secret of their calm. This looks like meekness: but it is a devilish pride. It may be boldly said, that it is a mark of a good man that one can make him angry. He is caring so much about things, and minding so much about his fellow-creatures, that he is easily stirred to indignation. So far from that being a fault, it is the sign of an ingenuous and wholesome nature. It is infinitely more respectful to a man that his acquaintance should be angry with him than that he should fancy him beneath even that tribute of his attention. A meekness whose source is in disdain can bring no blessing with it.

III. Nor is a third kind of meekness of moral

worth — that which is a mere dulness and torpidness of good nature — the fat serenity of a sluggish soul. There is no great merit in commanding one's temper if one have no temper to command.

Such counterfeits of the grace of meekness, ingenious and sustained though they be, will not for long deceive the observant. They have none of the impressiveness and charm of the virtue which Jesus blessed. Perhaps there is no quality of character more charming and more impressive.

The Prophet Isaiah reached a high level of inspiration when he described the Servant of the Lord in terms of this grace of meekness. "Behold My Servant, whom I uphold; Mine elect, in whom My soul delighteth: I have put My Spirit upon Him; He shall bring forth judgment to the Gentiles. He shall not cry, nor lift up, nor cause His voice to be heard in the street. A bruised reed shall He not break, and the smoking flax shall He not quench: He shall bring forth judgment unto truth." It is no wonder that the instinct of Christendom has seen that description fulfilled in "Gentle Jesus, meek and mild" — in the forbearing Lord "who when He was reviled, reviled not again; when He suffered, He threatened not." Just by such meekness Jesus has won the heart of the world.

There had been another in the history of Israel before Him who was known for his meekness also — Moses, the man of God. Take the Old Testament, and ask whose figure is the most dominant and majestic in it. The answer will be — It was the man of whom it is recorded that he was "meek above all the men which were upon the face of the earth." Like the greater Prophet, who was to come after him, Moses commands admiration because he was not aggressive and self-assertive, and (as we say in modern adjectives, unpleasant but often appropriate) he was not "pushing" and "loud" and "self-advertising." He also "did not strive nor cry, nor let his voice be heard in the street." The meekness of the man was his charm.

Take such a test for the people we know. Think of those who are always, as they say, "standing up for their rights" and refusing, as they express it, to be "put upon" — the people who are always looking out for slights and "determined to stand no nonsense" from any one — there is hardly a poorer spectacle in the world; and they are nearly always unsuccessful, losing the respect which they are so aggressively eager to gain. Contrast them with the meek whom we know — the gentlefolk at heart, whatever their birth may have been — who are not worrying about their dignity, and are too modest about their own powers to think that they have a claim to much distinction — the people who do not even like to speak too loudly in any company because it draws attention to themselves, and who would hate to obtrude themselves or make a show — the gentle, sensitive, shrinking souls, refined in thought and manner and speech, in whose very presence all violence is abashed and all self-seeking looks mean. Can we make such a contrast without understanding to the full what our Lord meant by the Beatitude, "Blessed are the meek"?

At our time when loudness and aggressiveness often seem the synonym of "modernness," and when indeed the nervous strain at which people live makes self-command more difficult and impatience a commoner fault than it used to be, it is good to hear and to give heed to that blessing upon the meek. All that is best in us leaps up to recognise its truth.

The reward which is promised in the Beatitude presents at first sight a greater difficulty: "Blessed are the meek; for they shall inherit the earth." Had it been heaven that was promised to the meek — that gracious world where the unselfish and holy have their home — then indeed the offer would seem assured of fulfilment. But it seems, at first, a paradox that the meek should find the rewards of earth. Such, however, was the promise of the Master, renewing an old declaration of the 37th Psalm which it is impossible to sublimate into any merely spiritual recompense. And is it, as a matter of fact, away from experience that in the long run, even in this world, it is not the "pushers" and the noisy who succeed? Violence has its day, but it is not always a long day. In those conversations in which Napoleon is recorded to have taken part during his banishment, there is one often-quoted saying of his: "Alexander and

Caesar and I founded great empires: but the empires perished because they were founded on force. Jesus Christ alone founded an empire upon love, and to this day thousands will die for Him." Whether Napoleon used those words or not, the sentiment in them is true. Examples of its truth are written large on the history of mankind. Think, for example, of South Africa. The story of our relations with that land is not on the whole a Ill-editable story. But there are aspects of it on which one can reflect with pride. Contrast, let us say, Cecil Rhodes with David Livingstone — the one a type of aggressive and self-confident vigour, the other an unwearied and unselfish worker for knowledge and freedom, and for Jesus Christ. When all for which the Rand millionaires stood has perished, and is remembered only as an ugly blot on the fair name of England, Livingstone's services to mankind will be a cherished and inalienable possession of our history. The meek will have inherited the earth.

The promise is not always fulfilled at once: it is an *heir* and not a possessor who is spoken of: an assured kingdom in the future, though it may be after many days. Yet the experience of men has been that the quiet and the thoughtful and the dutiful, in time came to their own.

Moreover, the real inheritance of the earth is very different from what hard men, in their eager ambition, suppose it to be. The conquerors can get the outside trappings of earthly possession; but what do they really gain even of the world they seek? While they are absorbed in their battles and their law-making, the homes and the hearts of the people are utterly outside their power. In a sermon to children, the late Dean Stanley of Westminster told of a grave-stone in the Abbey on which is written only these words: "Jane Lister, dear child, died October 7, 1688." Just at that date the public mind in England was filled with the rumour of revolution and of the coming of William and Mary to the English throne: but there in London, at the heart of the kingdom, two parents were thinking only of the blank in their home and the sorrow in their souls. In the last resort it is always so; kings and parliaments and rulers hardly touch at all the deepest elements of the life of the people. A man may seem to have inherited the earth when he has gained nothing more than some new anxieties and burdens to fill his days with pain.

"Dost thou wish to possess the earth?" asked St. Augustine once: "Beware, lest the earth possess thee." But the meek enter into a fuller inheritance of the earth, even the treasures of its honour and its love.

If a meek man, therefore, be ineffectual, it is not on account of his meekness, but on account of his weakness. A man like the patriarch Isaac, for example, lost much by undue concession in his old age: but he had made mark enough at his time by wise conciliation, and had settled terms of friendship and peace with his neighbours which no mere aggressiveness would have secured. For the Church of Christ, and for every Christian man and woman, it is a useful teaching yet, that the way to influence, permanent because worthy, is through the same channel of quiet persuasion and humble merit and the steady insistence of love.

They are advising other methods for the Church. Nothing pleases some of her critics in the unostentatious and old-fashioned ways. They will have advertisement and noise, and the methods of the theatre or the political platform. Such methods seem to succeed for a little, and crowds follow each new charlatan. But the demand for novelty and excitement exhausts itself, and heresy of doctrine or scandal of morals is the end of each new vagary of those who "lift up their voice in the street." The quiet, self-restrained ways of the Church are best. They are the most likely to secure a lasting success. Big things do not need to be shouted about. Life and death and destiny are persistent themes; and people feel that they approach them best, quietly, solemnly, without newspaper controversy and platform declamation. Therefore the future is with the Catholic Church — not, of course, only the Roman Catholic Church, but the Church of history and tradition — which seeks out the old ways and walks therein. "The meek shall' inherit the earth."

As a new type of character is being evolved in an age of competition and advertisement, it is worth while remembering also that the promise to the meek is not revoked in the twentieth century. David Hume once said: "Nothing carries a man through the world like a true, genuine, natural impudence"; and sometimes one is tempted to believe that Hume was right. In business and the professions and public life, there are successful men who seem to have no other qualification than that which is colloquially called "push." But is there more than a superficial truth in such a reflection? Whatever apparent success is found by such men, must it not be qualified and rendered nugatory to them by their association with the cultivated, the powerful in intelligence, and the refined in nature? Does it not become apparent to them (for they are not lacking in ability) that, after a little, they will be forgotten, and be as if they had never been, while ideals foreign to them are stamping their mark on society, and principles they could not grasp are changing the face of the world? What sort of an inheritance of the earth is that which must be loathed even while it is possessed, and is seen (if those men have eyes at all) to be but the possession of a day?

On the other hand, the meek — the holy and humble men of heart — find themselves at one with the eternal things, and in the fellowship of the saints, and in the brotherhood of Christ, and though they are not thinking of reward nor seeking it, for them the reward is sure — because natural, inevitable — the future must be with them, for they only are allied with the things that last

CHAPTER 4
THOSE WHO HUNGER AND THIRST AFTER RIGHTEOUSNESS

"Blessed are they which do hunger and thirst after righteousness: for they shall be filled."

— ST. MATT. V. 6.

A remarkable hymn, which once attained a great popularity, has in it the lines —

"Doing is a deadly thing.
Doing ends in death."

That hymn is suggestive of the famous comment of a Scotsman upon the Sermon on the Mount, that he did not think highly of the Sermon on the Mount; "there was too much morality in it."

A singular illustration of the same frame of mind was seen some years ago, when an edition of the

New Testament Scriptures was published which was known as the *Marked New Testament*. One or more red lines were drawn under every text which the editors thought of special importance. No mark at all appeared under the Beatitudes.

So far has one phase of Christian opinion passed from the characteristic teaching of Jesus Himself; so sadly has it lost His most characteristic note.

Contrast those rhymes about "deadly doing" with the words of our Master. "Every one that heareth these sayings of mine, and doeth them not, shall be likened unto a foolish man which built his house upon the sand." No condemnation of "deadly doing," is there. Indeed, it is impossible to go, with a mind unprejudiced and cleared from the accretions of a later theology, to the actual teaching of Jesus Himself without feeling that a passionate love of righteousness is through it. Morality, in its widest sense, is the very air it breathes. The Hebrew conscience has been called the "keenest religious instrument of the ancient world." A famous writer found in the word "righteousness" a summary of the whole Old Testament message. Jesus came not to destroy, but to fulfil that message. The very heart of His teaching is in the saying of St. John: "He that doeth not righteousness is not of God."

When, therefore, we hear Him offer a blessing upon those who "hunger and thirst after righteousness," we may be certain that there is no suggestion in His words of the doctrine called "imputed righteousness," or of any such doctrine which has come in after years to be prominent in Christian teaching. The Beatitude is a plain unequivocal blessing t upon those who do well — who try to live cleanly and be just to God and man.

There is, however, a note of passion in the words which removes them from the sphere of what in Scotland used to be called the "cold moralities." "Hunger" and "thirst" are primitive, fundamental appetites which every one understands. But middle-class people hardly understand them in their intensity of meaning. The men with the famished eyes who look in through the windows of bakers' shops and gloat greedily upon a plenty which they cannot share — they know the meaning of "hunger" and "thirst" as ordinary people hardly guess it. There is some suggestion of their eager desire in the "hunger and thirst after righteousness" over which the Beatitude is uttered.

A modern writer on religious subjects put this well when he said that "no love is pure which is not passionate, no virtue is safe which is not enthusiastic." It is such a love, such a virtue, which Jesus inculcates upon men.

Think of righteousness as He defines it, as He exemplified it on earth, as He personifies it still, and everywhere it has the power deeply to stir the heart. He defines Righteousness as an enthusiastic love of God and man — to love God with all our being, and our neighbour as ourselves. He exemplified righteousness in His own life as (1) a keen sympathy with the poor and sorrowful; (2) an antipathy just as keen to all Pharisaic superiority and unreality; (3) a lowly estimate of one's own need of honour and pleasure; and (4) a heroic devotion to duty beyond even what is normally expected of a man, so that an answer can be given to the question. What do ye more? But stirring as it is to the imagination to recall the figure of the righteous Lord and His consecrated life on earth, we have an inspiration that is loftier still in the contemplation of righteousness for ever personified in Him. As Dean Church finely said: "The Gospel calls us to the study of a living person and the following of a living mind." When, therefore, we hear the blessing upon those who "hunger and thirst after righteousness," it is no slavish adherence to the letter of a law, no cold morality which is enjoined. It is a burning attachment to the Fairest and the Holiest — a reverent remembrance of His beautiful life on earth, and an adoring worship of Him now glorified and crowned.

If any one ask why should we desire such a Righteousness, we do not argue over the matter. It is as natural that we should seek Christ as it is for "hunger" and "thirst" to desire to be satisfied, as natural as it is for the mind to think and the heart to feel. That is the charm of this Beatitude, and indeed of all of the Beatitudes, that they do not require to be argued for and defended. Once they were spoken, they became the indisputable and inalienable possession of the race.

Three aspects of the Beatitude, however, remain which demand some fuller treatment

I. First there is our Lord's teaching regarding the hopefulness of the human struggle. "Blessed are they which do hunger and thirst after righteousness: for they shall be filled." It has been the despair of the best men that their progress in the moral life has seemed so slow, and the goal so inaccessible. "Thy righteousness," said the Psalmist, "is like the great mountains." It is serene and most beautiful; but it is far away. It discourages and appals as much as it fascinates. Many have thought of Jesus so — disconcerted and abashed in His presence rather than allured to follow in His steps. The ideal will always have in it some such aspect of awe. But it is the teaching of Jesus that every one who really wishes to be good will be good; those who seek the supreme righteousness and whose souls are athirst for God, will be satisfied with the object of their desire.

It is the law of this world that environment answers to need. The eye seeks light and finds it; the body seeks food and finds it; so will the hungry soul be satisfied.

Here once more we have the experience of multitudes to say Amen to the teaching of our Master. It may be that there never were so many people at any time as there are at our time who have found the supreme satisfaction of the soul just through this avenue of the appetite for Righteousness Our Lord said that His spirit would convict men "of sin and righteousness and judgment" At other periods of the world's history, the sense of sin and, it may be, the fear of judgment, have brought men to themselves and to Christ Through these gateways they have reached the Highest. But the sense of sin is less acute at our age, and certainly the fear of judgment is a less formative emotion; fewer people find the conviction of their personal sinfulness or the dread of eternal suffering to be a road to the Saviour's heart. But there never was so humane a spirit in any community. There never was a greater longing for the abolition of old tyrannies and the establishment of justice between man and man. Never did the general heart respond more readily to the claim of unselfish and generous ideals. Never in all the ages were more men led to the Lord Jesus, just because they were convicted of "Righteousness," and saw in Him the realisation of every dream of justice and compassion which they had cherished. Because they "hunger and thirst after righteousness," they are "filled with all the fulness of God."

II. The second aspect of the Beatitude which demands our notice is its recognition of the place of aspiration in character. The road to character is generally described as through act and custom and habit But there is more in life than act and custom and habit. There are efforts, deep desires, and high ambitions, aspirations, impulses, Teachings forth of the nature which have never perhaps crystallised into acts, but which are most meaningful in the making of a man. It is after all a "hunger" and "thirst" which are blessed, and not an attainment, an achievement, a possession. If a true judgment on human life is to be passed, it must be by one who knows not only what we have done, but what we have honestly tried to do. There is many a glorious failure which has left a more permanent mark for good upon the soul than a hundred easily won successes. So the brightest charm of this Beatitude is not its promise of the perfect attainment of Heaven, where they serve in righteousness without a flaw, but its blessing upon the toilsome way along which, with many a stumbling step, we press forward towards the goal.

> "Not on the vulgar mass
>   Called 'work,' must sen-
>   tence pass.
> Things done, that took the
>   eye and had the price;
> O'er which, from level
>   stand,
> The low world laid its
>   hand,
> Found straightway to its
>   mind, could value in a
>   trice:

"But all, the world's coarse
        thumb
    And finger failed to plumb,
So passed in making up the
        main account;
    All instincts immature,
    All purposes unsure,
That weighed not as his
        'work,' yet swelled the
        man's amount:

"Thoughts hardly to be
        packed
    Into a narrow act.
Fancies that broke through
        language and escaped;
    All I could never be,
    All, men ignored in me,
This, I was worth to God,
        whose wheel the pitcher
        shaped."

"The great thing in this life is not having, but wanting: turning from all earthly havings to thirst for the unattained. Life's possibilities lie infinitely beyond life's realisations. Having is a limited thing which in possessing we transcend. A deep, persuasive sense of lack touches the infinite; every true thirst of the being resolving itself into a thirst for God."

Blessed are they which do hunger and thirst after righteousness.

III. But perhaps our third reflection is of most practical value. How is such a hunger and thirst after righteousness to be stimulated? How in the multitude of desires, rational and irrational, by which the will is swayed, are those better impulses to be cultivated and given sway? We desire much, fiercely and persistently. Base appetites usurp large rooms of the heart. Ambitions for honour without desert, and reward without the duty that has earned it, and popularity without the service to our brethren which is its one worthy excuse— such desires move restlessly through our minds. How shall we learn to hunger more for righteousness than for ought else? There is a sermon on this theme by a divine eminent in his day. Dr Leckie of Ibrox; and he had no better suggestion to offer than that we should read much of good biography. "Lives of great men" are indeed good reading — far better than fiction, just because they have that singular charm of the authentic about which Carlyle used to speak so much, and which most of us have ourselves experienced. A good biography of a really good man must stir a generous admiration, must excite at least some desire to emulate the hero's virtue and services. Therefore there is no better reading for the young, whose minds are formed so much by examples, and who assimilate a precept for life so much more easily and permanently when it is presented in concrete form. There is no need to detract from Dr. Leckie's praise of a good biography as a stimulus to the hunger for righteousness. No one could read of Wilberforce, or Shaftesbury, or Livingstone without being, at least for the time, on a loftier plane of being.

But the shallower thought of his sermon may be set beside a strangely impressive discourse by one of the great preachers of the world. Horace Bushnell has a sermon which bears the title, "Christ regenerates even the desires." He dealt with the incident when the Sons of Zebedee came to Jesus and asked Him to give them whatever they wished. Bushnell showed the folly of their random request and the strange psychological problems which open before the mind which would seriously consider the worth of human desires. And then he proceeded to show how James and John, the inconsiderate and reckless, were yet so moved in after days by their fellowship with Christ, that even their desires were transfigured and regenerated. The whole secret of the government of the nature is disclosed by one of them — St John — when he says: "Whatsoever we ask we receive of Him, because we keep His commandments, and do those things which are pleasing in His sight." "He was in God's order, and now all his desires went to their mark."

The habit of prayer, the new love of the Lord which so adjusts the nature that all the gusty inclinations of the soul are laid at rest; above all, the companionship with Christ which moulds our minds to His and makes us insensibly take His type — these methods, and the discipline of Providence, are the ways in which the desires, which are at the back of consciousness and outside the reasoned government of the will, can be conformed to the highest, and men may learn to "hunger and thirst after righteousness."

But of them all there is none so effectual as the love of Christ, which thinks of Him as the friend and companion of the soul, and desires to be with Him as an exile pines for home. There is a letter by David Gray, the Scottish poet, which is among the saddest things in literature. Gray was a lad of promise and of a fine nature. He yearned for a life of letters, and nothing would serve him but to leave his home near Glasgow and adventure upon the great world of London, there to make his fame. He fell into a consumption: he was poor and dying; and this is what he wrote to his parents: —

"Torquay, *Jan.* 6, 1861.

"DEAR PARENTS, — I am coming home — homesick. I cannot stay from home any longer. What's the good of me being so far from home and sick and ill? O God, I wish I were home, never to leave it more. Tell everybody that I am coming back — no better, worse, worse. What's about climate, about frost or snow or cold weather, when one's at home? I wish I had never left it. I have no money; and I want to get home, home, home. What shall I do, O God? Father, I shall steal to you again, because I did not use you rightly. Will you forgive me? Do I ask that?... I have come through things that would make your heart ache for me — things that I shall never tell to anybody but you, and you shall keep them secret as the grave. Get my own little room ready — quick, quick: have it all tidy and clean and cosy against my homecoming. I wish to die there, and nobody shall nurse me except my own dear mother, ever, ever again. O home, home, home I"

Blessed are they who hunger and thirst after Righteousness, which is Christ, in such a way as that: for they shall be filled.

CHAPTER 5
THE MERCIFUL

"Blessed are the merciful: for they shall obtain mercy."

—ST. MATT. V. 7.

"Blessed," "Blessed," "Blessed" — the iteration of the gracious word as the Beatitudes go on is significant of much. When, at the close of His earthly life, Jesus passed into the Unseen, it was "while He blessed His disciples that He was parted from them." A chain of blessing bound together the beginning and the end of His ministry. It was all a positive Gospel which He taught. Not fear nor self-interest was the motive which He stirred. He appealed with the winsomeness and the joy of goodness.

Those who have once heard the Commination

Service which is used in the Church of England on Ash Wednesday, the first day in Lent, are not likely to wish ever to hear it again. The minister is directed to read the words, "Cursed is the man that maketh any carved or molten image, to worship it." "And the people shall answer and say, Amen." Then the minister goes on: "Cursed is he that curseth his father and mother," and the response is made, "Amen." Eight other curses follow, and an address of terrifying severity. One feels in a different world from that hillside where a benignant and beautiful Being smiled upon the kind souls that loved Him and were His friends, and in the glorious sunshine of an Eastern day told them of the inner joy of goodness: "Blessed," "Blessed," "Blessed."

The Beatitudes, and not the Commination Service, contain the characteristic note of the Christian Gospel. The stern sanctions of the law indeed remain, and the awful facts of life in which sin and punishment are inextricably bound together. But the inspiration of character is no longer in the recital of things forbidden: it is in an ideal that is positive, spiritual, unworldly, and most fair.

It is this sense of being at the heart of Christianity when we read the Beatitudes which has made them fill so large a place in the minds both of friends and of foes of our faith. It is a curious fact that two writers who have been among the most influential forces in literature during the past generation, Tolstoi and Nietzsche, have each directed a keen interest upon the Beatitudes, Nietzsche in a bitter and mocking hatred, Tolstoi in a subservience of reverent obedience almost slavish in its literalness. There could not be a better illustration of the feeling, which we all experience in some degree, that here, in this part of our Lord's teaching, we are dealing with the crucial questions: we are touching the live heart of the Gospel of Christ.

It may be that the blessing on the merciful is of all the Beatitudes the most characteristic, the most suggestive of the original elements of the new religion. It concentrates on itself the attention of friend and foe of the faith. When people speak familiarly of "a Christian spirit," they nearly always mean a merciful and forgiving spirit. When a great writer like the author of *Ecce Homo* turned to a study of the Christian Gospel, he found in this subject of Mercy the theme of almost half his book. The attraction of the Christian ideal to myriads of men — and its repulsion for some others — just lies in this, that we name our Master the Man of Mercy.

The misunderstanding of this Beatitude both by friend and foe would, however, have been to some degree removed had there been a proper insistence on the fact that every side of human excellence is not suggested by the blessing on the merciful.

Probably our Lord thought it unnecessary to utter a Beatitude on common Honesty. That, and the great virtues which the moralists describe as the Cardinal Virtues — Justice, Prudence, Temperance,

Fortitude — are assumed to be the furniture of a good man's mind. Much of the current criticism of the Christian ideal would have been seen to be unnecessary had it been taken for granted that Jesus was dealing with reasonable men, and expecting their common sense to supply the scaffolding of His ideals. This very grace of mercifulness were worthless if it were a mere thoughtless and unregulated emotion. Long before the day of our Lord, the Psalmist had shown how in a complete character "mercy and truth are met together, righteousness and peace have kissed each other."

It may be difficult to draw the boundary between the sphere of mercy and of truth, and to show what a man's course should be who wants to be kind, but is trying also to be just. Most human graces are not like a rectangular State of the American Union, whose frontier is drawn in straight lines. They are rather like the counties of old England, where the boundaries follow, here the bendings of a river, and there the margin of a lake. Definitions are usually difficult where the line of duty is concerned. But Mercy and Truth meet each other easily enough in life when the practical reason is unhampered by casuistry and a wise benevolence has its way.

Truth, of course, saves Mercy from being a maudlin sentiment like that which snuffles in a theatre over make-believe sorrow, but is unrelated to the exigencies of life.

But the office of Truth is not to be a mere check

upon Mercy. "Why do you hate that man?" said one to Charles Lamb; "you do not even know him." "Of course I do not know him," answered Lamb; "for if I knew him I probably should not hate him." It is so that a better understanding of a human life, with its difficulties and manifold disadvantages, often takes the bitterness out of the judgment we might pronounce. There is no happier proof of this than in the feet that mercy is a grace which grows with growing years. The young are often hard. Having seen little of life and its trials, they pronounce swift censures on the failures. But as we get older we are more considerate. Mercy and Truth meet together.

Here is the explanation also of those unrelenting judgments which even the kindest are apt to pass on some offences. Sir John Seeley quotes a modern novelist as saying, "There are some wrongs that no one ought to forgive, and I shall be a villain on the day I shake that man's hand." Though the words seem cruel and unchristian, there is a feeling not dissimilar which many of us cherish. Not to speak of those nearer to us, there is a feeling that Sir Walter Scott's Varney and Dalgarno, or Thackeray's Marquis of Steyne, or Shakespeare's Iago, ought not to be forgiven — at least that we could not bring ourselves to forgive them. Is not the whole secret in this, that their characters being what they were, we could not believe in their being really penitent and asking forgiveness? If only we could be assured of that — if, that is, we could really get at the truth about them, would resentment continue unabated? Would a Christian heart forget the lesson of seventy times seven?

The main consideration to keep in our minds is, that the mercy of which Jesus spoke is no mere pity or sympathy divorced from intellectual judgment and deprived of moral weight. It proceeds upon the use of the minds God has given us. "Mercy and truth are met together."

According to our Lord's teaching in two memorable parables — the Good Samaritan and the Unmerciful Servant — Mercy is manifested either in active benevolence and works of charitable relief, or in a placable, generous, and forgiving temper.

a. In a sorrowful world there is much need for Good Samaritans. The plentiful abuses which disfigure every society, even the most civilised; the cruelty of man to man, and of man to the lower creatures; and those degrading and demoralising conditions which seem to be the inevitable accompaniment of industrial competition, call out for helpers. There are many unselfish souls in every community trying their best to remove or alleviate such evils. On them the blessing of the Lord is pronounced. Every visitor of the sick and the poor, every manager of a hospital, every director of a charity, has a claim to some share in this Beatitude.

Such a merciful spirit is most seen within the Christian Church; but the law of mercy, and the blessing on it, is irrespective of all creeds. "Blessed are the merciful" — where-ever they may be.

b. The parable of the Unmerciful Servant — that story of the man who was hard and vindictive towards his inferior at the very time when his heart should have been melted by the recollection of his own forgiveness — has set in a lurid light the sin of an implacable temper. Within the realm of such teaching lies many an instructive word for the conscience of Christian men and women. Many who would not break the more formal commandments are lamentably lacking here.

We find our associates in some enterprise very trying and difficult to do with. If our minds work quickly we are impatient with the low level of ability which is common. In boards and committees and Church courts, and in the intercourse of business, we encounter men and women of irritable tempers and absurd prejudices, people who take offence where no offence is meant, and exaggerate careless words into ridiculous importance. If we have a talent for pungent clevernesses we are tempted to its frequent employment; and our whole critical attitude to life tends to be that of satire. Blessed, indeed, are we if gentler graces save our souls. Let thoughts of home and wife and children be often with us to sweeten things. Let some ministry to the sick and the poor keep sweet the human sympathies. When our frame is the hardest let us try to look at the face of Jesus, such as convention has painted it for us and as we know it must have been. It is told of Charles Dickens — who surely of all English writers has most earned the Beatitude upon the merciful — that he wrote concerning a criticism of his on Tom Hood which had appeared in the *Examiner*: "The book is rather poor: but I have not said so: for Hood is poor too, and ill besides." What a new and most tender charm would come both into letters and into life were such a merciful spirit commoner than it is.

"Blessed are the merciful: for they shall obtain mercy": —

A learned commentator on this promise has warned us to look for no barter in it, as if the Lord had said, "If you treat another man kindly he will be kind to you." That, he points out, is not the real state of affairs, not what happens in actual life. The most merciful Man the world has known was murdered by an ungrateful race. Yet surely, though such a reward does not always come, there is sufficient experience to warrant the promise even of an outward and a present reward of mercy. A lady in a very prominent place in what is called Society has had a wonderful tolerance extended to her, and an explanation was once given of it. "I have known Mrs K. all my life, and I never heard her say a hard word against any one." There are surely among the acquaintance of most of us some such men and women who are popular and sought after almost for no other reason than that their thoughts of others are kindly, and bitter criticisms are never on their lips. Merciful, they obtain mercy.

Can we not think of others whose own savage and merciless judgments have made their life a long unhappiness and surrounded them with enemies? Everyone knows the epitaph that is set over the grave of Jonathan Swift in Dublin. "Here lies the body of Jonathan Swift, where his fierce indignation can tear his heart no more." Those who can recall that morose and savage spirit, that truculent and fierce career, are not willing to banish into another world the reward of a gender virtue, "Blessed are the merciful: for they shall obtain mercy."

In yet another sense than in the kindly judgment of our contemporaries the merciful obtain mercy every day. They train themselves to generosity by the use of generosity. The act goes before the habit and the frame of mind. By pitying they learn to be pitiful. Serene and happy lives the man who has learned to think well of his friends and of the world he lives in, who is not looking for faults or delighting in the mistakes or offences of his fellows, whose mind instinctively takes a generous and a gentle view, and whose heart is for ever overflowing in the little tendernesses which make life gracious and beautiful. The source of happiness to others, that man is happy himself. As Portia said in the famous passage, which every preacher on Mercy must quote, he is "twice blest." Then, last, when our minds expand beyond the sphere of our earthly striving and see such a man facing the unseen world, where "the works of earth are tried by a juster Judge than here," we know that he enters the presence of the merciful Father as no alien to His spirit, as no stranger to the courts where pity and love have their home. "Blessed are the merciful: for they shall obtain mercy." The bond of fellowship, which a life of love has forged, is manifest when the illusions of earth and the misunderstandings of men have disappeared.

At this point a resemblance- between the Beatitudes and the Lord's Prayer, which often suggests itself to the student, becomes most evident. "Forgive us our debts," we are taught to pray, "as we forgive our debtors." Even as early as the time of St. Chrysostom there were men, he tells us, who would not say that prayer in its completeness, and omitted the phrase "as we forgive our debtors." They dared not ask to be forgiven as they forgave. As a man of hard and unrelenting temper says the familiar words to-day, as with a grudge against some offender in his heart, and a lurking passion for revenge, he asks to be forgiven as he forgives, the dreadful impiety of the petition may well startle his conscience into some self inquiry, and the dread of the punishment he is invoking may well send him to seek reconciliation, and it may be friendship anew.

"Blessed are the merciful: for they shall obtain mercy." They shall obtain it; but they need to show it no more. It is one of the strangest pictures, and it is almost the saddest picture, of a world of redeemed and sanctified men that one of the gracious virtues of life is needless any longer in that happy land. For sorrow and sin are both done away, all that excites compassion and all that cries for forgiveness and lenient judgment, in the new transfigured world, have disappeared, and Mercy is swallowed up in the great broad river of Love.

CHAPTER 6

THE PURE IN HEART

"Blessed are the pure in heart: for they shall see God."

—ST. MATT. V. 8.

"Mysticism," said John Wesley once, "is just heart religion." Here in the Sixth Beatitude of Jesus is the essence of mysticism — its aim to see God; and its method, by purity of heart. But, though one calls such a type of religion by a name which suggests theology and which has been appropriated to describe a certain class of thinkers, mysticism is really the religion of the great masses of mankind. The permanent elements of religion come to most men under a mystical guise. It is not evidences and arguments which are their origin, but the universal instincts of the human soul. Unlettered men perceive them; poor sufferers on their painful beds, hardly capable of consecutive thought, cling to them with an assurance which reason could never bring; little children have known them better than the wise. "Wouldst thou plant for eternity?" said Carlyle, "then plant into the deep infinite faculties of man, his fantasy and heart. Wouldst thou plant for year and day? then plant into his shallow superficial faculties, his self-love and arithmetical understanding. Religion is planted in that which is deepest in man. Therefore it lasts: and despite any passing phase of doubt or criticism it will last for ever.

"It is with the heart that a man believes." The two most famous churchmen of France in the twelfth century were St. Bernard of Clairvaux and Peter Abélard. Of the two, Abelard had by far the more alert, the subtler, and the more brilliant mind. He was a thinker and a teacher, while Bernard was only a prophet. But who can doubt which of the two saw most of things divine, and which of the two has left for us to-day the more precious legacy? The criticism and dialectic of Abelard, in advance of his time as they were, have perished from the memory of men, and his name is chiefly associated with a somewhat sordid love story; while, ever as men sing Bernard's hymn, "Jesus, the very thought of Thee," they will know the meaning of the Beatitude, "Blessed are the pure in heart: for they shall see God."

It would indeed be wrong to fancy that any slight is thus cast upon the great disciplines by which the learned theologians reach their results. The Beatitude gives no honour to mental sloth. A man often says, "I know," when he only means, "I am too lazy to prove." The criticism of sacred books and the labours of philosophy have a place in furnishing "a reason for the hope that is in us." Yet it is not by such a path that we reach "the hope that is in us." The simplest and most untutored soul may find it, if only his heart be pure.

We believe that God made man in His own image, and that man's soul is a mirror in which the mind of God is reflected.

> "Speak to Him, then, for He
> heart, and spirit with
> spirit can meet;
> Closer is He than breathing,
> and nearer than hands
> and feet."

It is perhaps impossible to explain the methods by which man thus sees his Maker: this confident leap of the whole nature — thought, emotion, will — in one sublime affirmation. It is perhaps wisest for most to say that here is an experience — a fact of consciousness as sure as any in life. If one seeks an analogy for it, some analogy may be seen in our apprehension of poetry, or beauty, or music, or human love.

There is a memorable passage in Plato's *Apology*, in which Socrates tells the result of his questioning of the poets about their methods. "Taking up some of their poems which seemed to me most elaborately finished, I questioned them as to their meaning. I am ashamed, O Athenians, to tell you the truth; however, it must be told. Almost all who are present could have given a better account of them than they by whom they had been composed. I soon discovered this, therefore, with regard to the poets, that they do not effect their object by wisdom, but by a certain natural inspiration."

Ask any great interpreter of nature about the meaning of the outside world for the soul of man — read Wordsworth — and you will find the same phenomenon: "Sensation, soul, and form all melted in him"; "Words needed none; his spirit drank the spectacle." Beauty and sublimity came in an immediate apprehension utterly apart from the logical understanding. It is as impossible to describe in words, yet quite as sure a fact of consciousness, as the love of man for woman, or of woman for man — that great source of human happiness, that turning-point of the human tragedy, which yet has no terminology which can be quoted without exciting a smile.

In some such way might one illustrate the vision of God. Man, because he is a spirit, is able to commune with the Great Spirit; and we know the Father as by love and fellowship we know an earthly friend. This is the wonderful truth, so revolutionary, so far reaching, which is at the root of the Beatitude, "Blessed are the pure in heart: for they shall see God."

If, then, man's nature be the mirror in which the Divine is reflected, how essential it becomes that the mirror should be clean.

A man whom the present writer knew once spent a winter at Rome. He had introductions to the inner circle of what is known as "Black" society — the friends and supporters of the Roman Catholic Church. The man saw nothing of the antiquities of the famous city, and gathered no intelligent views even regarding its modern life. He could talk fluently upon only one theme — the system of lotteries! He had looked on everything with a gambler's eye. Thus, from the highest to the lowest interests of life, it is true that as a man is he sees. The gravest heresy is not error of doctrine, but impurity of life.

Such a reflection may often bring comfort to parents who are distressed to see their children — young, anxious-minded, inquiring — fall into doubt or even into denial of those things which are the most precious in life, the great truths of our faith. If a youth be sincere and simple-minded, and truth-loving and a clean liver, he will come through the shadows which rest for a time upon his belief and will emerge into the clear day. It is natural, and almost inevitable, that if a man keep himself in the atmosphere of God — in the life of righteousness — he will not always fail to recognise the Great Companion who is by his side.

Such an experience is abundantly confirmed. "Who shall ascend into the hill of the Lord?" asked the Psalmist, "who shall stand in His holy place?" "He that hath clean hands and a pure heart," was the answer. Remember any time in our national life when the best in our people has been awakened — such a time as that of the last great war— when the fire of patriotism burned clear, and sympathy and pity for the fallen and wounded soldiers were thrilling all hearts, and the country stood consciously in the presence of the great critical things of life: was it not true that our religious life also was keener, and we saw more manifestly the hand of Providence in history? With a purified heart we learned to see God?

Or let a man ask himself when his own faith was most vivid and he looked on life most in the light of God's purity and truth? Was it not just when he was at his best: when sorrow had softened him or gifts of love had made him feel how good it was to be alive? Was it not when he stood by the cradle of his little child or by the coffin where the dear dead lay? Was it not when he had had the grace to overcome a great temptation or turn aside from a course he knew to be evil though it allured? Was it not when he was most a man, that then also he believed most firmly in God and saw Him near? It is with such experience that life has confirmed the blessing on the pure in heart.

Or why is it that, on the whole, women have been more devout believers than men, and have followed the Master with a simpler faith? Is it not just because, as a rule, women are not so coarse in thought or conduct as men, and they have found the blessing on the pure?

There is no use in illustrating the teaching more. But the closer we get to the facts of life the more certain we become of this great message of Jesus to men.

It is better to ask what is the road to purity of heart? How shall the condition of this Beatitude be gained?

The answer must often be in terms of that indirection which is so often the method of Jesus. Do not seek happiness, and you will be happy. Do not think about purity, and you will be pure. Christina Rossetti, when she set herself in one of her books to write about the Seventh Commandment, began with these suggestive words: "One legitimate mode of treating our present subject, and it may be not the least profitable mode, is to turn our hearts and thoughts away from it."

It is never well to allow the imagination to dwell on evil things, even in the very process of condemning them. So strange a thing is human nature that a leering delight can be found in the exposure and punishment of wickedness, and a man may be a satyr in the guise of a militant saint. For most people it is better to occupy themselves more with positive good than with attacking wickedness. "Whatsoever things are pure. . . think on these things." The way to a pure heart is by the road of absorption in unselfish duty.

But a certain standard of simplicity and sincerity can be consciously set before one and sedulously cultivated. A quaint illustration of such a type of mind may be found in a letter which George Washington wrote to his friend Governor Morris, who was going to Europe. Among other commissions, Washington asked him "to buy him in Paris a flat gold watch; not the watch of a fool or of a man desirous to make a show, but of which the interior construction shall be extremely well cared for, and the exterior air very simple." It is not a bad standard for a man as well as for a watch — "the interior well cared for, the exterior air very simple." Washington himself was a noble example of such purity of heart. And the qualities of which his letter gave so quaint and significant a suggestion, have in some measure marked all men of the really highest type.

Prayer is, however, the great appointed instrument by which purity of heart is retained or recovered. "Create in me a clean heart, O God," we are taught to ask. Here we are on the same level of ascertained experience, on which it is wise to keep while we are discussing a theme where the risk of unreality or sentimental vagueness is great. Let any man put to himself the question. How is the bad in me most subdued? How do I reach the loftiest aspirations? How do I come near the heart of God? It is by the avenue of Prayer.

When Jesus promised to the pure in heart that they should see God, He did not fix the time of the blessed vision. Is it to be here on the homely earth, or only beyond, where they gaze with other clearer eyes? Surely we should answer — and all that has been said has implied it — even here we may see God. "He that hath seen Me hath seen the Father," said our Lord Jesus. All good and holy men and women have some testimony to give of their knowledge of the heart of God in Jesus Christ. In the last century there were two teachers of the Church of England who live in a very sacred memory for their sincerity and guilelessness, their generous enthusiasm, their purity of heart. They were Dean Stanley and Charles Kingsley. Of Kingsley it is recorded that on his deathbed he seemed to have some glimpse of the Beatific Vision, for he exclaimed, "How beautiful is God." And the last sermon which Stanley preached was on the text, "Blessed are the pure in heart: for they shall see God." He preached it on the 8th July 1 8 8 1; and he died on the 1 8 th of the same month. The last words of that sermon speak of "the single eye and the pure conscience which are an indispensable condition of having the doors of our minds open and the channel of communication kept

free between us and the supreme and eternal foun-
tain of all purity and of all goodness." Thus, even
here on earth, the pure in heart are blessed with
such an inward gift of God as "eye hath not seen, nor
ear heard, nor hath it entered into the heart of man
to conceive." But we may well believe, also, that a
fuller vision is yet to come. "Here we see through a
glass darkly, here we know in part." But when,
through the training of the years the faculties of the
spirit have been disciplined and enlarged, when
death has removed every disturbing medium of
sense, the Divine which is so often shadowy and in-
distinct will glow before surprised and adoring eyes
in a beauty of which now we can hardly dream, and
the Providence over life which speaks to us now so
often only with hints obscure and difficult to inter-
pret, will win us to an awed recognition of its mercy
and its love.

> "I'll blest the hand that
> guided. I'll bless the heart
> that planned.
> When throned where glory
> dwelleth, in Immanuel's
> land."

"Then we shall know even as we are known." "It
doth not yet appear what we shall be; but we know
that when He shall appear we shall be like Him, for
we shall see Him as He is."

> "Father of Jesus, love's
> reward.
> What rapture will it be,
> Prostrate before Thy throne
> to lie,
> And gaze and gaze on
> Thee."

Well may St. John comment after He had made the glorious promise of that Vision of God: "Every man that hath this hope in him, purifieth himself even as He is pure."

CHAPTER 7
THE PEACEMAKERS

"Blessed are the peacemakers: for they shall be
called the children of God."

—ST. MATT. V. 9.

There is something arbitrary in most
attempts to trace a connection between the
Beatitudes, and to discern in them an inter-
related scheme of character. But when one deals
with the blessing upon the Peacemakers it is abundantly evident that its true place is after the blessing
on the pure in heart. St. James, with his practical
judgment, saw this when he declared that "the
wisdom that is from above is first pure, then peaceable." In more picturesque language the same connection of thought is made manifest in the Epistle to
the Hebrews, where that romantic figure of early

history, Melchisedek, is described as "first king of righteousness, and after that king of peace."

Every one who reads the Bible in the light of his own heart can find experiences which make that connection between righteousness and peace sufficiently clear. If a family is what it ought to be, there is authority and a well-ordered home life as the basis of the family happiness. Because, in too many modern homes, indulgence has come before rule, and parents have thought of what would please before they settled what was right, the old home life is in danger of decay. In a school, in a university, there will be no good work done unless discipline be steadily placed before teaching. Right relations must be established before happy results will come. It is such familiar things of life which have made the solemn doctrine of the Atonement, with all its difficulties of statement, appeal to men's minds as consonant with things as they are. First righteousness, then peace: explain it how you will, goodness must first be vindicated before man can be reconciled with God or his neighbour or himself.

This connection of the Beatitude on the Peacemakers with that which immediately precedes it, makes it clear that if a man is to be of any use in mediating peace to the world it must be because his own heart has been brought into conformity with the highest. "First keep thyself in peace," said St Thomas à Kempis, "and then thou shalt be able to keep peace among others." The source of such a serenity of a calm and self-controlled spirit is in fellowship with God in Jesus Christ our Lord.

The God of Peace is the noble New Testament name of the Father. Seven times in the Epistles, St. Paul recurs to the phrase the "God of Peace," and he sets the gift of peace in the midst of the benediction in the thrice Holy name. St. Paul's summary of the interests of the Kingdom of God is "righteousness, peace, and joy in the Holy Ghost."

It is indeed true that in an earlier revelation the Lord had been described as a man of war: and there was a truth also, not merely temporary, in that awful name. Mr. Disraeli once answered a deputation of the Peace Society by saying to them, "I believe in the God of Hosts"; and if we see an overruling providence in history, we also must recognise that, even as great storms clear the air of the world and make it a wholesomer place to live in, so it has been through human strife that a way has often been found to a peace with which honourable and right-minded men could be satisfied. When Benjamin Franklin said that "there never was a good war or a bad peace," he offended against a just interpretation of history; he uttered a sentiment as absurd as if he had said that it never was good to arrest a criminal, and it never was bad to let the wicked have their will. As the world is constituted, force must sometimes be used on the side of righteousness, and God can be called now, as in the times of early revelation, the God of Hosts.

Yet that is not, nor ever has been, his characteristic name. He is the God of Peace. When the fulness of glory was manifested among men it was in the person of the "Prince of Peace," at whose birth the angels sang of "peace on earth," and who, ere His passing hence, left as a legacy to mankind a gift of the "Peace" which had been His own.

If, then, a man's nature be in fellowship with God as He is revealed in Jesus Christ, the trend of his character also must be toward conciliation, co-operation, brotherhood, love. He must see that the spirit of contention and strife is no worthy offering to the Lord whom he worships and would serve.

It is strange that, even in the Church of Christ, there have been men who did not see this. There have been — there are — Churchmen who are firebrands and men of war from their youth. Aggressiveness is in the very cut of their face and in the note of their voice in the most ordinary talk. Their boast is that of Alan Breck in Stevenson's famous story, that they are "bonny fechters," and their happiness is keenest when controversy is high. God forbid that anyone should say that these are the worst of men. They are better than the sluggards, who are only peaceable because, as they say, they "like a quiet life": they are better than the cowards who will not risk the unpopularity or the unpleasantness that the defence of truth or the overcoming of iniquity will ever involve. But they who merely revel in disputes have much to learn before they win to the spirit of Christ or gain the blessing which He offers to the Peacemakers, that they shall be called the Sons of God.

It was this feeling, doubtless, which made a great teacher like St. Augustine content to accept the translation of the Beatitude as it is given in the Vulgate, "Blessed are the Peaceable." If a man's own nature has not ceased from warfare, he is ill equipped for that ministry of reconciliation to which they are commanded who are in fellowship with Christ.

The correct translation, however, is, "Blessed are the Peacemakers." And a larger call is made upon Christian men than only to find peace in their own hearts. We must be ambassadors of Christ's peace to the world.

I. What of controversy in politics, in the Church, in social life? Controversy must exist while minds are diverse; and in many respects it is wholesome. A Peacemaker can engage in it with a clear conscience. His love of peace, however, will regulate the methods with which controversy is carried on. All irrelevant personalities will be hateful to him, and he will argue to convince and not to stab or wound. Sure of his own position, he yet will try to understand the position of his adversary. And deliberate misinterpretation or appeals to prejudice will form no part of his methods. Difference of opinion so expressed need make no breach of friendship, need injure no human relationship. It is probable that when Barnabas and Paul differed, it was a real quarrel, and they parted less good friends than they had been — though a happy reconciliation was to come. But when Peter had been tampering with principle at Antioch, Paul "withstood him to the face," because he was to be blamed; and we do not read that their honest argument affected the terms on which the two great and magnanimous souls stood to each other. In a democratic country like ours great honour is due to those who keep the temper of controversy good, and who carry the spirit of the Peacemaker into public life with its dignifying, sweetening power.

II. The Industrial Community, so often cursed with stupid strikes and labour wars, is learning also, and will learn better, the value of the Peacemaker. There is hardly a better test of a big man than that he is naturally sought for as an arbitrator, trusted by both sides for his judgment and fairness of mind. To an increasing extent such arbitrators will win a position in modern life. There are few better names than that of the chairman of a Church court in Scotland. He is called the Moderator.

Such moderators in civil affairs, calming loud-voiced or angry altercation, bringing order out of confused dispute, themselves unruffled, impartial, are most useful members of any community. The machinery of life is apt to get heated while it works so swiftly. Blessed are they who oil the wheels: Blessed are such Peacemakers.

III. When it comes to interference with private or

domestic quarrels, a wise man will show the prudence which tells him that the way to peace is often the policy of Non-Intervention. A meddler is often a muddler. He who intervenes between relatives, and especially between husband and wife, has often to discover that he has helped no one, and has only added to the discomfort of all, not excluding himself. The author of the Book of Proverbs does not always rise to the highest level of inspiration, but he had a shrewd knowledge of human life when he said: "He that passeth by and meddleth with strife not belonging to him, is like one that taketh a dog by the ears." Vanity has made some people fancy that they were called to the office of Peacemaker in cases when their wisdom would have been to abstain.

It must not, however, be supposed that Christian folk have no duty at all in these particulars. In our social life there are two courses especially which every good man or woman should resolutely follow.

(a) The first is to hate all tale-bearing and malicious gossip. No worse disturber of the peace of homes exists than the idle retailer of unpleasant criticisms. There are three levels of conversation. The highest is talk about ideas; the second highest is talk about things; the lowest is talk about persons. Beyond this lowest level many people hardly care to rise. It is not that they are malicious only, though some evil spirits delight in any gossip which will cause pain. It is chiefly that they are empty-minded and thoughtless, and do not realise the harm that their reckless chatter works. Against all such evil gossip a Peacemaker sets his face like a flint. Among the seven things which the Book of Proverbs says God hates, one is "He that soweth discord among brethren."

If a bad story comes to a Peacemaker he will refuse to believe it while he can, and he will abstain from repeating it to the last. If, however, some story of kindness and heroism and self-denial comes to him, he will blaze that abroad. For the world is a better place for its good tales of human brotherhood and love.

(b) In quiet ways also a man of a peaceable spirit can do much to compose troubles and to disseminate the spirit of consideration. A man comes to us ruffled and out of temper on account of some slight he has suffered: we can ask him — as Dr. Johnson asked Boswell in such circumstances, to "bethink himself how the matter will appear twelve months hence." Or he shows us an angry letter he has written, full of clever jibes and thrusts and bitternesses: we can urge him not to send the letter for a day or a week; we can divert his mind to other matters till the annoyance which prompted it has passed away.

The Peacemaker's influence in such respects is moral rather than intellectual. One can rarely argue a man out of a temper. One can often compose him out of it in the presence of better and kinder thoughts. Such thoughts melt the frozen heart as the sunshine of spring is the solvent of the snow.

Blessed indeed are such Peacemakers. By their very presence they are continually, though unconsciously, making people think better of themselves, of humanity, even of God. They live in the presence of ideals which make angry disputes seem mean. And the peace which keeps their own hearts and minds radiates a benediction upon all they know.

"Blessed," said our Lord, "are the Peacemakers: for they shall be called the sons of God." Sons of God indeed they are: but also they will be recognised and owned and called by their right name. It may not be at the first. Then the keen fighter for his side arouses the cheers of his fellow combatants, and the protagonist is the hero of the crowd. It may not be at the first. Then the Peacemaker is called other names than a son of God; he is called "Trimmer," or even "Traitor." But when the dust of battle sinks, and the noise and tumult of war die into silence, and men ask (after a century) who were the figures which stand out from the time as most venerable, the best servants of their generation? it will not always be the redoubtable champions of a party — though to them also honour is due — it will be the holy and humble men of heart who were thinking of larger interests than those of a sect or a political cause, who where looking to the welfare of the State or the Church of the Lord Jesus Christ, who were striving for that unity for which the Saviour prayed, and who loved peace and laboured after it with all the power of their generous hearts.

Such are the men — it would be easy to name some of them — in the Church and in the State whom, as we look back over the years, we venerate the most. Jesus the Son of God was also the Prince of Peace, and we call those men "sons of God" because they were like Him. Now that all branches of the Christian Church in Scotland, as in Canada and Australia, are awake to the scandal of our unhappy divisions, and the evils wrought by the long war which Christian folk have waged with one another, we have no use for fighters, and quarrellers, and bitter speakers, and cruel hinters any more. We are looking with an affectionate longing for the man who will repair the broken walls of the city of God, and earn for himself the blessing which is the Peacemaker's due.

When a small company, of whom the writer was one, buried Archibald Forbes, the distinguished war correspondent, whose life had been one long adventure, and who had seen as much fighting as any man of his time, we chose as the hymn to sing over him, ere his worn-out frame was laid to its long rest, the verses —

> "No longer hosts encoun-
> tering hosts
> Shall crowds of slain
> deplore;
> They hang the trumpet in the
> hall.

And study war no more."

It was not only the thought of the war-worn veteran's rest that came to one's mind as thus we sang; it was the vision of the strifes which have desolated society, the controversies which have been the scandal of the Church, the disputes which have alienated the tenderest ties of home — all stilled, composed, for ever at an end. Must it be only Death that shall work such a consummation? Is it not possible even here in our pleasant land to see Jerusalem, the city of peace, reared once again fair as ever, ere her battlements were hurled down in internecine struggles and her streets defiled with the blood of brethren? We live in times when the Peacemaker is coming to his own. If not in our time, or our children's, yet for the Church and for society the sons of God will make strange and happy things to be.

> "Down the dark future
>   through long generations
> The sounds of war grow
>   fainter and then cease,
> And like a bell with solemn
>   sweet vibrations,
> I hear the voice of Jesus
>   Christ say, 'Peace'."

CHAPTER 8
THE PERSECUTED

"Blessed are they which are persecuted for right-eousness' sake: for theirs is the kingdom of heaven."

— ST. MATT. V. 10.

It is the difficulty of all expositors of the Beatitudes that any exposition seems unnecessary.

"To gild refined gold, to paint
    the lily,
To throw a perfume on the
    violet,
To smooth the ice, or add an-
    other hue

> Unto the rainbow, or with
> taper-light
> To seek the beauteous eye of
> heaven to garnish,
> Is wasteful and ridiculous
> excess."

Some such feeling gives pause to the homilist who ventures to make more plain and convincing the Master's words: "Blessed are the merciful," or "Blessed are the pure." The eighth Beatitude, however — the blessing on the persecuted — makes no such immediate and obvious appeal. For that reason, as well as for the reason that it is not so plainly spiritual as the others, it is not always reckoned in the number of those sayings of Jesus which we call His Beatitudes.

Yet it well deserves a place beside the other seven. It is really as spiritual as the rest Though it seems to refer to outward condition rather than to character, it must not be supposed to teach that persecution itself makes a man blessed: everything depends upon the motive for which the suffering is met and the spirit in which the suffering is borne. "It is the cause," said St. Augustine once, "which makes the martyr." Our Lord would have uttered no benediction on those servants of His who provoked a useless persecution, and, in the pride of a self-conscious virtue, threw away their lives in vain. The blessing on the persecuted is a blessing on the inward and spiritual graces of wisdom and fortitude and faith.

If there be some truth in the criticism that this Beatitude does not so immediately as the others convince with the clear-cut simplicity of an aphorism, and our Lord Himself needed to amplify and explain it, yet, when it does reach the mind and the heart, it is as characteristic of the Master's teaching as any of the rest.

This is a word of Jesus which our distance from His time and His surroundings makes less vivid in its appeal to our imagination. When we say "persecution" we think of an unpleasant letter in the newspapers, or the rudeness of some acquaintance, or the petty spitefulness of society. When Jesus said "persecution," He spoke to twelve men of whom only one was to die in his bed. If we would understand what being "persecuted" meant when Jesus spoke of it, we should read the eleventh chapter of 2 Corinthians, with its breathless record of the sufferings of St. Paul. It was in view of such penalties of their discipleship that Jesus pronounced His followers blessed, and exhorted them to "Rejoice."

Here is the great wonder of it. Every other leader of men, who has had a heart at all, has grieved over the distress which he was bringing upon his friends even in a good cause. Mazzini deplored the desolation and sorrow which the glorious struggle for freedom was to spread over Italy. But Jesus saw the torturer and the executioner stand beside His well-beloved, and He said, "Rejoice, and be exceeding glad." "Blessed are they which are persecuted for righteousness' sake." Far from being unworthy of a place among the Beatitudes, this blessing on the righteous sufferer is one of the most startling pronouncements as to the meaning of the Gospel.

Those who read the great evangelic prophecy which runs through the fortieth to the sixty-sixth chapters of Isaiah have ever been accustomed to find in it a subtle interpretation of the sacrifice of Jesus. These chapters might almost be summarised in the saying, "Blessed are they which are persecuted for righteousness' sake." When Jesus Himself said, "If any man will come after Me, let him take up his cross and follow Me," He showed that persecution in some sense was the normal condition of the Christian. St. Timothy was told the same truth by his leader in later days, "All that will live godly in Christ Jesus shall suffer persecution." There is not a note of depression in one of these utterances. To suffer for righteousness' sake, and to be glad of it, is the account of Christian experience which seems to them all the natural and the happy lot.

How shall we bring this down to the conditions of modern life, when the martyr fires are no longer kindled, and museums hold the iron boot and the thumb-screws? Do men, as a matter of fact, still suffer persecution for righteousness' sake, and find it blessed?

There is no more certain fact of life than that

they do. There are some sections of society, at the top and at the bottom, where every condition is antagonistic to what is altruistic, generous, refined. No one doubts that there are large circles of society where it is difficult to be a Christian, and where the man or woman who tries to be a Christian suffers for it. Even the very presence of an unworldly piety excites dislike in certain bosoms. When it proceeds to be aggressive, as it must when it is genuine, a fierce and deadly hatred is aroused.

The forms of persecution change: its essence remains unchanged. "The honourable and religious gentleman," a slaveholding member of Parliament nicknamed William Wilberforce. Innuendo and all the arts of the traducer and defamer are wielded still by the enemies of righteousness when their vested interests are attacked and their selfish or vicious pleasures are denounced. Such opposition is the lot of every reformer. The weak and the unprincipled yield before it The dread of unpopularity breaks their will. There is nothing sadder in the public life of our country than the haunting note which runs through the speeches of many politicians in all parties — the note of fear. These men speak, not as men who are thinking out great questions and telling the result of their thought in plain speech, but as men who have an eye on the ballot-box and will risk anything rather than the loss of a vote.

If the Church also has to some extent forfeited the confidence of the country, it is because she also has been afraid of persecution, because for fear of causing alarm, or of making good people angry, her ministers and her teachers have kept silent over matters which every educated man knows have seriously affected her attitude to the Bible and to other solemn matters of the faith. "The fear of man bringeth a snare." And in every department of life it is one of the commonest enemies of righteousness.

That is one fact of experience. The other is this: that the men who are able to overcome such fear and to suffer persecution for righteousness' sake enjoy a satisfaction, an exhilaration, a zest of life well worthy of being called Blessedness. Paul and Silas singing in the prison-house — their limbs in chains and the hard floor for their bed, yet with the joy in their hearts of being on the right side and fighting for it — they are, for ever the type of that highest happiness of which this Beatitude tells. Our human nature has sorrowful features in it, and there are many indulgence seekers and shirkers and cowards. But there is also something heroic in human nature which responds to the call to hardship.

What is the best appeal to win men to be missionaries to the heathen? Shall we tell them of a good salary, and a warm climate, and frequent furloughs? We shall never get a man worth sending by such an appeal. But bid them think of a lonely life amid fever and squalidness, and of a slow disheartening struggle to bring to Christ a native people sunk in superstitions and bound by horrible customs, and we shall get the right men to seek such a life of hardship.

Thank God, the Church has got them. Hard work and unpleasant surroundings and opposition are not real deterrents to any profession, to any demand upon human energy. Often, indeed, they are the opposite: and a man is never more himself, and never happier, than when he is fighting with his back to the wall against heavy odds.

> "Come one, come all, this
> rock shall fly
> From its firm base as soon
> as I."

There are, perhaps, few of us who have not had some such exhilarating experience and who do not know how true the Lord's words are: "Blessed are they which are persecuted for righteousness' sake."

The fuller elaboration of this Beatitude makes it easier than in the case of the other seven to trace the elements of gladness and satisfaction which are promised.

I. First: theirs is the kingdom of heaven. Once more, as to the poor in spirit, the assurance is given that the most precious rewards of life are not a distant gleam of glory, but the present possession of a faithful soul. "The way to heaven is through heaven, and all the way to heaven is heaven, and only the heavenly shall enter heaven." The man who is persecuted for righteousness' sake knows himself as in alliance with the spiritual forces which are the redemption of the world.

His very persecution tells him that; for it makes him recognise that he is making something of it and winning his way. As a ship passes out from the harbour heads, and meets the open sea, she tosses and rolls amid the great ocean billows; but every buffet of them is a message of her conquest over obstacles, every strain and pitch and plunge tell of her triumphal march towards her goal. As St. Paul saw the furious mob at Ephesus or the murderous Jews at Antioch or Iconium, he must have taken a quiet comfort from their rage. It told him that, whether they liked his teaching or not, at least they were thinking of it, and studying it, and had the sense to see that it was revolutionary, and that he was "turning the world upside down." Their persecution made him a hundred times happier than the polite insouciance of the Athenian crowd.

There are two kinds of opposition — the opposition of the stone wall which the cannon shot knocks to splinters when it strikes, and the opposition of the earth redoubt into which the balls sink with a dull thud and against which they make hardly any impression at all. It is the second kind of opposition which is the more formidable. If a man sees himself hated and reviled and persecuted, he knows at least that the power of the truth he holds dear is being felt and understood; and, since he cares for nothing so much as for that, a happy man is he. There is no experience better described as being in "the Kingdom of Heaven."

II. Our Lord goes on to say, "Blessed are ye when men shall revile you, and persecute you, and say all manner of evil against you falsely, for my sake": and surely He suggests a very deep source of human joy by the thought that we are privileged to suffer something for Him. All love wants to sacrifice, and looks for an opportunity to delight itself by suffering. The awkward lad who spends a week's wages on a gift to his sweetheart; the mother who sits up all night beside her sick and peevish child, seeking no more than the opportunity of lavishing care and affection on the unresponsive creature: these are on the ascending scale of love, which, when it reached the highest, gave a well-beloved Son for a world of sinful men. The purest happiness is in this. "Remember," said St. Paul, reporting words of the Master which the evangelists somehow had strangely missed — "Remember the words of the Lord Jesus, how He said, It is more blessed to give than to receive." It is such a blessedness which the persecuted know: they have the opportunity of doing something — or bearing something — for Christ's sake, and it is the proudest privilege which mortals know.

III. Rejoice, and be exceeding glad, the Master went on to say, "For so persecuted they the prophets which were before you." Every sufferer for righteousness' sake is set in a great line — the goodly fellowship of the prophets, the noble army of martyrs, the saints of all ages (as of our own) who have seen that active goodness awakens the animosity of worldly men and brings trouble back to brave and faithful souls. The story of the world's ingratitude is a black page; and in it there is one spot, the blackest, where the name of the Crucified is written. But the letters on it are all of gold. "He loved His race: He tried to teach and help and save it; and He suffered for it" — that is the record of some of the world's best. "Look back along the great names of history," wrote Mr. Froude in one of those *Short Studies* which will remain, in the judgment of the wise, among the foremost essays in the English language; "there is none whose lot has been other than this. They to whom has been given the really highest work on earth to do — whoever they were, warrior, philosopher, legislator, poet, priest, slave — one and all their lot has been the same: the same bitter cup has been given to them all to drink." As humble men and women meet petty persecution, and are called by foolish nicknames, and feel the multitudinous pin-pricks of social disagreeablenesses, is it not something for them to feel that they also are of the company of the world's greatest? "So persecuted they the prophets which were before you."

Such reverence for the holy and brave who have gone before us, such loyalty to their memory, such comradeship with their aims, is one of the loftiest incentives to the Christian life.

> "O the way sometimes is low,
> And the waters dark and
>   deep,
> And I stumble as I go.
>
> But I have a tryst to keep;
> It was plighted long ago,
> With some who lie asleep.
>
> And though days go dragging
>   slow,
> And the sad hours grave-
>   wards creep,
> And the world is hushed
>   in woe,
>
> I neither wail nor weep,
> For He would not have it so,
> And I have a tryst to keep."

IV. They little know the mind of the Master, who shut out from His teaching the last element of blessedness which this Beatitude contains — a promise for the future. "Great," said He, "is your reward in heaven." Not in the Sermon on the Mount only, but often in other discourses, he called His disciples' thought beyond the scene of our earthly striving to a serene land where a throne is set for the conqueror and a crown is brought for his brow, and a glory not of earth is his everlasting portion. We know not what outward conditions are represented by language so figurative, so deeply tinged with the colours of earth: but it is idle to banish from the message of Jesus the hope for the righteous of a reward.

His best and most unselfish servants gloried in it. "If we suffer," wrote St. Paul to his pupil and associate — "if we suffer we shall also reign with Him." Those who understand the human heart at all, see nothing sordid in the dream. For what is the reward — what is the crown of glory — which such holy souls have believed was waiting them beyond the grave? They can but express it in terms of material things, and hint at it vaguely in the gorgeous imagery of the senses: but it was no selfish enjoyment they were looking for: no "enjoyment" in any sense which ordinary thought attaches to the word. It was to be with Christ: in some way, which even fancy refuses to outline, to see His blessed face, to dwell in the presence of the ineffably Good and Fair. Because Jesus was the despised and rejected of men, because men reviled Him and persecuted Him, and spoke all manner of evil against Him falsely, therefore all who are persecuted for righteousness' sake feel that, in such an experience, they are being disciplined into His likeness, and they rejoice at their hard lot, not because one day it is to be made easier, but only because it is the way which leads them nearer Him.

Does a student love less the profession he has chosen, and for which he is being trained, because he hopes some day to exercise it nobly for the good of his fellows, and to make some mark in the world through it before he dies? Does a man love less his promised wife because he looks with eager and happy expectancy to the marriage day when he can claim her for his own? Shall we be such bloodless servants and followers of Christ that we are stirred by no vision of the home country of His saints, and find no alleviation of the hardships and self-denials which His service may entail in His own assured promise of a reward, "a hundredfold now in this present time, and in the world to come life everlasting."

Those moralists deal with other creatures than with men, who bid us banish from our minds even a beautiful and unselfish conception of heavenly happiness. The Lord Himself knew man's nature, and He animated faith and hope by His benediction on the persecuted, "Rejoice and be exceeding glad; for great is your reward in heaven."

APPENDIX

No one should approach an exegetical study of the Beatitudes without some knowledge of the questions of Biblical Criticism which are involved. For example: how are the eight Beatitudes of St. Matthew related to the four of St. Luke? It was maintained by a great father (St. Ambrose) that the two sets are virtually identical. But the whole question needs working out. It is sufficient to guide the reader to the learned discussion of this aspect of the Beatitudes in Hastings' *Dictionary of the Bible*, the Extra Volume, page 15 and ff.; and the *Dictionary of Christ and the Gospels*, page 176 and ff.

Every exegetical commentary on the Gospels devotes some space to the Beatitudes. Such a book as Wendt's *Teaching of Jesus* sets the Beatitudes in their relation to the whole message of our Lord.

There is no more suggestive treatment of these themes in English than the relevant chapters in Bishop Gore's book, *The Sermon on the Mount*. But the late Dr. Oswald Dykes is fuller and more practical in his *Manifesto of the King*. In a volume of sermons by the late Dr. Leckie, entitled *Life and Religion,* seven discourses are devoted to the Beatitudes. (Like many others, Dr. Leckie reckoned that there were seven, not eight, sayings deserving of the title.) The late Professor A. B. Bruce devotes two chapters of his popular yet very able work, *The Galilean Gospel,*to the Beatitudes. Simpler but not less helpful are the four sermons in the late Dean Stanley's *Sermons to Children.* A ponderous volume, entitled *The Charter of Christianity,* published in 1886 by Andrew Tait, D.D., LL.D., a Canon of the Church of Ireland, gives 76 of its 628 pages to the Beatitudes. Bishop Boyd Carpenter has a volume of sermons on the subject, *The Great Charter of Christ*; and Bishop C. J. Ridgeway has a volume, *The Mountain of Blessedness.*

On the word Beatitude itself, which does not occur in the Bible, see Trench's *Study of Words.*

On the proper rendering of μακάριος see Montefiore's *The Synoptic Gospels,* from the point of view of scholarship, and from the far more important point of view of spiritual insight, the 9th chapter of the Second Book of *Sartor Resartus.*